Somewhere Between

*Three
Rehearsals*

and the

Performance

by
Mark Nicholls

This first edition published in Australia in 2019 by:

Prahran Publishing
P.O. Box 2041, Prahran, Victoria, 3181

© Copyright Mark Nicholls 2019

Mark Nicholls has asserted his legal and moral right under the Copyright Act 1968 to be identified as the author of this work.

Published by arrangement with
Prahran Publishing, Australia.

All rights are strictly reserved.

No part of this publication may be reproduced, stored in a retrieval system or transmitted, in any form or by any other means, without the publisher's prior permission in writing. Copying of this script for performance reasons is also strictly prohibited by law, either in whole or excerpts from.

This book is sold subject to the condition that it shall not, by way of trade or otherwise, be lent, resold, hired out or otherwise circulated without the publisher's prior consent in any form of binding or cover other than that in which it is published and without similar condition, including this condition, being imposed on the subsequent purchaser.

Every reasonable effort has been made to trace copyright holders of material reproduced in this book, but if any have been inadvertently overlooked the publishers would be glad to hear from them. The story, all names, characters, and incidents portrayed in this book are fictitious. No identification with actual persons past or present, places, buildings, and products is intended or should be inferred.

ISBN 978-1-922263-04-9 Paperback
ISBN 978-1-922263-05-6 eBook

Dewey: 822.4

A catalogue record for this book is available from the National Library of Australia

Performance Licensing and Royalty Payments

Mark Nicholls retains control of both the amateur and professional stage performance rights of this play. No unauthorised performance should occur without the express and written permission of the playwright.

Restriction of Alteration

There shall be no modifications of any kind to the play including deletion of dialogue (including objectionable language), changes to characters gender or names, title of the play or music without the express and written permission from the author.

Sound and Video Recordings

This play may contain stage directions to include the use of music, video or other sound recordings either in part or in whole. The author and the publisher have not sought the right to use such content and performance rights permission should be obtained seperately. Permission to record audio and video recordings of all performances must also be explicitly given by the author in writing.

Author Credit

Performance rights approval requires credit be given to Mark Nicholls as the sole and exclusive author of the play. This obligation applies to the title page of every program or other advertising material distributed in connection to this play. The author's credit should appear immediately under the title of the play on all published material, and alongside no other individual. Font size of credit cannot be less than 50% of the largest letter used in the play's title.

Please email info@prahran.press
for all performance enquiries.

Dedication

For Anika Ervin-Ward.

Present at the creation

About the Playwright

MARK NICHOLLS has been performing on various Melbourne stages since the age of six and has an extensive list of credits as a playwright, composer, singer, actor, producer and director. He is Senior Lecturer in Cinema Studies at the University of Melbourne where he has taught film since 1993.

He is the author of *Lost Objects of Desire: The Performances of Jeremy Irons* (2012), *Scorsese's Men: Melancholia and the Mob* (2004) and recently published articles on Italian Cinema, Powell and Pressburger's *The Red Shoes* and Sergei Diaghilev's celebrated company, The Ballets Russes.

Mark is a film critic and worked for many years on ABC Radio and for *The Age* newspaper, for which he wrote a weekly column between 2007 and 2009.

He lives in Melbourne with his partner, Ali Wirtz, and their two sons Oscar and Carlo.

Series Preface

I wrote these plays for only one reason, to perform them. I publish them here, therefore, somewhat reluctantly. They were never written to be read on the page by anyone but a treasured posy of performers that I trust to help me rescue them from it. They were certainly never conceived of as works of anything so respectable as literature. Nevertheless, I have found two reasons to overcome my reluctance and my usual roguish prejudice against readers and writers in favour of performers and punters. One reason is that putting these plays into print provides the opportunity for the most engaged of those who saw and heard them to revive and revise the experience. The other reason is archival. I wish to leave a permanent, if inadequate, record of the facts of their production over a decade, in a private space in Melbourne, for the benefit of both a small, dedicated paying audience, and for a smaller band of compulsive show-folk.

Writing these plays for the talented actors, musicians and backstage characters whose creations are recorded here, and having the privilege of working with these artists to produce them, has been the most satisfying occupation of my otherwise horrendously charmed and fascinating life.

Now that they have had their blessed release in print, these plays are beyond the concern of any motivation I had to write them. Read them, o curious one, and work it out for yourself! One motivation I will record, however, rests in the inspiration generously given by those who worked on and attended these cosy performances, and so brought their privileged, fleeting moments of theatre securely into being.

About the Play

We first planned *Somewhere* as a longish short film. The storyboards for this unproduced masterpiece are full of shots of Caerwen Martin cycling through Carlton apparently drowning in Ravel's *Piano Trio in A Minor* and completely untroubled by local regulations concerning the wearing of helmets. I too was drowning in Ravel when I wrote it and that particular trio was both the inspiration for the play and the originally intended performance for which three rehearsals were so foolishly deemed sufficient. I had hoped to do this film entirely with real musicians and the fact that cellist, composer and actor, Caerwen Martin walked into our lives as the first auditionee during the first audition promised success. It proved tricky, however, to get the right instruments played professionally in the hands of the right actors, so this dream of collaboration was soon abandoned. So too was the heterosexual nature of the central love story. I always seem to know so many wonderful female actors and very few blokes, so the idea of this ending up as a vaguely gay (or at least bi-curious) romance was, what is often referred to as, a no-brainer. In the end, that other bloke, Maurice Ravel, and his trio were also abandoned, but not before the idea of shooting this as a film was itself confined to bottom desk drawer.

I have always wanted to direct *As You Like It* and tried to do so three times before this play let me have something of a go at it. Rosalind is one of Shakespeare's great characters – she is such an inspiring mover and shaker and a gift for any actor and her/his director. If I ever hear the banished Duke speak "so gently" to bratty Orlando without being moved in my heart of hearts, I will say goodbye to love for ever. Like Claude Debussy, I have always been stimulated by the musical possibilities of *As You Like It*. In between my second and third attempts to produce it, I wrote the songs *O My Faith* and I once sang long songs of sorrow in the period of my life which was also marked by the genuine ambivalence that comes with the birth of children.

The idea for the setting of *It was a Lover and his Lass* might as well have come to me in a pub. *Under the Greenwood Tree* is given the sort of torch-song treatment that might have been offered to Rita Hayworth to sing in a casino bar long after closing – or Frank Sinatra anywhere, anytime. None of these songs would have got off the keyboard without Caerwen Martin's meditative cello solos or her vocal stylisations as Rosalind, and those of Madeleine Swain as Celia. Martin and Swain really are a director's dream team and the years of productive work that followed at Rear Four were largely based on the foundation they provided.

If I stole the idea to form this company from anyone, it was undoubtedly from Anika Ervin-Ward, herself and a mover and shaker to whom Rosalind herself would defer as an acknowledged master.

A note on the play within the play

In Shakespeare's *As You Like It* (1600) the cousins Rosalind (Ellen) and Celia (Lana) are banished from court by the reigning duke, Celia's father. Seeking out the exiled Duke, Rosalind's father, they repair to the Forest of Arden where they complicate matters by assuming new identities; Celia as Aliena, the shepherdess, and Rosalind as Ganymede, a boy fair and of female favour. In the rustic retinue of the exiled duke, they re-encounter Orlando (Glenn), a dull but attractive Romantic hero, for whom Rosalind once expressed a degree of sexual enthusiasm when she saw him prevail in a wrestling match. If Orlando is bright enough to know that she is really a girl, he seems to enjoy her just as much as a boy, at least until the inevitable Shakespearean moment comes – as it never comes in life – when all these confusions are put right.

Characters

ELLEN: thirty-two, an actor/musician, mother and wife

LANA: thirty-four, an actor/musician without particular responsibilities

GLENN: thirty-two, an actor/musician, and manic promoter

Passages in the text taken from Shakespeare's *As You Like It* are indicated by reference to the name of Shakespeare's character in the play, e.g. "ELLEN: *[As ROSALIND]* I was seven of the nine days out of the wonder..." Two songs from Shakespeare's play, *It was a Lover and his Lass* and *Under the Greenwood Tree* have been included, as they were set to music by the author, with minor alterations to the original lyrics.

Somewhere Between Three Rehearsals and the Performance was first performed at Rear 4, Clifton Hill, Victoria on the 3rd of July 2008 with the following cast:

Ellen	Caerwen Martin
Lana	Madeleine Swain
Glenn	Mark Nicholls
Director	Mark Nicholls
Associate Director	Anika Ervin-Ward
Co Producer	Alison Wirtz

Act 1 - Scene 1:

It is the first week of autumn. Soon we will see the three actor/musicians working together. If we could tell anything from the interaction between the three we would know that they don't know each other very well at all. We would also know that the GLENN is running the show, and too many others at the same time to give anything but momentary attention to this one. ELLEN and LANA may not approve of this but they have worked in such a way before and certainly will again. What is important to know about them is that ELLEN is about to fall into the grip of a short infatuation with LANA and that the brief history of this performing trio without a name will be the backdrop for the building and then the dousing of that fire. LANA may see this is on the cards, in fact she may look forward to the possibility every time she accepts an invitation to perform in a group like this. Whether ELLEN knows it now is unimportant as once she does she will never remember a time when she didn't. Nothing of this, of course, shows in the performance, which is without blemish.

> *For now GLENN and LANA turn on the lights and enter a rehearsal space somewhere in Carlton, Victoria. There is a piano in the space and GLENN goes to it, opens it and sits down. LANA drops her bag beside it and pulls out her script. We cannot hear the few words that pass between them before they start work on the song, the first number in the 'As You Like It' song cycle written by GLENN.*

GLENN: OK?

LANA: Yeah.

LANA: *[sings]* It was a lover and his lass,
With a hey, and a ho, and a hey nonino,
That o'er the green corn field did pass,

GLENN: *[sings]* In spring time!

LANA: When birds do sing, hey ding a ding,
Sweet lovers love the spring,
Sweet lovers love the spring.

Between the acres of the rye,
With a hey, and a ho, and a hey nonino,
These pretty country folks would lie

GLENN: In spring time!

LANA: When birds do sing, hey ding a ding,
Sweet lovers love the spring,
Sweet lovers love the spring.

	This carol they began that hour,

                This carol they began that hour,
                With a hey, and a ho, and a hey nonino,
                How that a life was but a flower,

GLENN: In spring time!

LANA: When birds do sing, hey ding a ding,
Sweet lovers love the spring,
Sweet lovers love the spring.

GLENN: And therefore take the present time,
With a hey, and a ho, and a hey nonino,
For love is crownèd with the prime,

LANA: In spring time.
When birds do sing, hey ding a ding,
Sweet lovers love the spring,
Sweet lovers love the spring,
Sweet lovers love the spring,
Sweet lovers love the spring.

Sweet lovers love the spring.

Towards the end of the song ELLEN rushes in, highly self-conscious of the fact that she is late for her first rehearsal for anything in nearly ten years. Flustered, she takes the first chair she sees and throws her things on it. While she is muddling with her script, still standing, LANA takes ELLEN's bag and puts in on the other chair, much to ELLEN's horror. Following the end of the song, LANA begins to read passages from 'As You Like It' from her script.

LANA: *[As CELIA reading]*
Why should this a desert be?
For it is unpeopled? No:
Tongues I'll hang on every tree,
That shall civil sayings show:
But upon the fairest boughs,
Or at every sentence end,
Will I Rosalinda write,
Teaching all that read to know
The quintessence of every sprite
Heaven would in little show.
Therefore Heaven Nature charged
That one body should be fill'd
With all graces wide-enlarged:
Thus Rosalind of many parts
By heavenly synod was devised,
Of many faces, eyes and hearts,
To have the touches dearest prized.
Heaven would that she these gifts should have,
And I to live and die her slave.
[To ELLEN as ROSALIND] Didst thou hear these verses?

ELLEN is still not quite ready and is caught off guard.

ELLEN: *[As ROSALIND]* O, yes, I heard them all, and more too;

LANA: *[As CELIA]* But didst thou hear without wondering how thy name should be hanged and carved upon these trees.

ELLEN:	*[As ROSALIND]* I was seven of the nine days out of the wonder before you came; for look here what I found on a palm-tree. I was never so be-rhymed since Pythagoras' time, that I was an Irish rat, which I can hardly remember.
LANA:	*[As CELIA]* Trow you who hath done this?
ELLEN:	*[As ROSALIND]* Is it a man?
LANA:	*[As CELIA]* And a chain, that you once wore, about his neck. Change you colour?
ELLEN:	*[As ROSALIND]* I prithee, who?
LANA:	*[As CELIA]* O Lord, Lord! it is a hard matter for friends to meet; but mountains may be removed with earthquakes and so encounter.
ELLEN:	*[As ROSALIND]* Nay, but who is it?
LANA:	*[As CELIA]* Is it possible?
ELLEN:	*[As ROSALIND]* Nay, I prithee now with most petitionary vehemence, tell me who it is.
LANA:	*[As CELIA]* O wonderful, wonderful, and most wonderful wonderful! and yet again wonderful, and after that, out of all hooping!
ELLEN:	*[As ROSALIND]* Good my complexion! dost thou think, though I am caparisoned like a man, I have a doublet and hose in my disposition? One inch of delay more is a South-sea of discovery; I prithee, tell me who is it quickly, and speak apace. I would thou couldst stammer, that thou mightst pour this concealed man out of thy

mouth, as wine comes out of a narrow-mouthed bottle, either too much at once, or none at all. I prithee, take the cork out of thy mouth that may drink thy tidings.

LANA: *[As CELIA]* So you may put a man in your belly.

ELLEN: *[As ROSALIND]* Is he of God's making? What manner of man? Is his head worth a hat, or his chin worth a beard?

LANA: *[As CELIA]* Nay, he hath but a little beard.

ELLEN: *[As ROSALIND]* Why, God will send more, if the man will be thankful: let me stay the growth of his beard, if thou delay me not the knowledge of his chin.

LANA: *[As CELIA]* It is young Orlando, that tripped up the wrestler's heels and your heart both in an instant.

ELLEN: *[As ROSALIND]* Nay, but the devil take mocking: speak, sad brow and true maid.

LANA: *[As CELIA]* I' faith, coz, 'tis he.

ELLEN: *[As ROSALIND]* Orlando?

LANA: *[As CELIA]* Orlando.

ELLEN: *[As ROSALIND]* Alas the day! What shall I do with my doublet and hose? What did he when thou sawest him? What said he? How looked he? Wherein went he? What makes him here?

	Did he ask for me? Where remains he? How parted he with thee? and when shalt thou see him again? Answer me in one word.
LANA:	*[As CELIA]* You must borrow me Gargantua's mouth first: 'tis a word too great for any mouth of this age's size. To say ay and no to these particulars is more than to answer in a catechism.
ELLEN:	*[As ROSALIND]* But doth he know that I am in this forest and in man's apparel? Looks he as freshly as he did the day he wrestled?
LANA:	*[As CELIA]* It is as easy to count atomies as to resolve the propositions of a lover; but take a taste of my finding him, and relish it with good observance. I found him under a tree, like a dropped acorn.
ELLEN:	*[As ROSALIND]* It may well be called Jove's tree, when it drops forth such fruit.
LANA:	*[As CELIA]* Give me audience, good madam.
ELLEN:	*[As ROSALIND]* Proceed.
LANA:	*[As CELIA]* There lay he, stretched along, like a wounded knight.
ELLEN:	*[As ROSALIND]* Though it be pity to see such a sight, it well becomes the ground.
LANA:	*[As CELIA]* Cry 'holla' to thy tongue, I prithee; it curvets unseasonably. He was furnished like a hunter.

ELLEN: [As ROSALIND] O, ominous! he comes to kill my heart.

LANA: [As CELIA] I would sing my song without a burden: thou bringest me out of tune.

ELLEN: [As ROSALIND] Do you not know I am a woman? when I think, I must speak. Sweet, say on.

LANA: [As CELIA] You bring me out. Soft! comes he not here?

Enter GLENN [As ORLANDO]

ELLEN: [As ROSALIND] [Aside to CELIA] I will speak to him, like a saucy lackey and under that habit play the knave with him.
[To Glenn [As ORLANDO]] Do you hear, forester?

GLENN: [As ORLANDO] Very well: what would you?

ELLEN: [As ROSALIND] I pray you, what is't o'clock?

GLENN: [As ORLANDO] You should ask me what time o' day: there's no clock in the forest.

ELLEN: [As ROSALIND] Then there is no true lover in the forest; else sighing every minute and groaning every hour would detect the lazy foot of Time as well as a clock.

GLENN: [As ORLANDO] Where dwell you, pretty youth?

ELLEN:	*[As ROSALIND]* With this shepherdess, my sister; here in the skirts of the forest, like fringe upon a petticoat.
GLENN:	*[As ORLANDO]* Are you native of this place?
ELLEN:	*[As ROSALIND]* As the cony that you see dwell where she is kindled.
GLENN:	*[As ORLANDO]* Your accent is something finer than you could purchase in so removed a dwelling.
ELLEN:	*[As ROSALIND]* I have been told so of many: but indeed an old religious uncle of mine taught me to speak, who was in his youth an inland man; one that knew courtship too well, for there he fell in love. I have heard him read many lectures against it, and I thank God I am not a woman, to be touched with so many giddy offences as he hath generally taxed their whole sex withal.
GLENN:	*[As ORLANDO]* Can you remember any of the principal evils that he laid to the charge of women?
ELLEN:	*[As ROSALIND]* There were none principal; they were all like one another as half-pence are, everyone fault seeming monstrous till his fellow fault came to match it.
GLENN:	*[As ORLANDO]* I prithee, recount some of them.
ELLEN:	*[As ROSALIND]* No, I will not cast away my physic but on those that are sick. There is a man haunts the forest, that abuses our young plants with carving 'Rosalind' on their barks; hangs

odes upon hawthorns and elegies on brambles, all, forsooth, deifying the name of Rosalind: if I could meet that fancy-monger I would give him some good counsel, for he seems to have the quotidian of love upon him.

GLENN: *[As ORLANDO]* I am he that is so love-shaked: I pray you tell me your remedy.

ELLEN: *[As ROSALIND]* There is none of my uncle's marks upon you: he taught me how to know a man in love; in which cage of rushes I am sure you are not prisoner.

GLENN: *[As ORLANDO]* What were his marks?

ELLEN: *[As ROSALIND]* A lean cheek, which you have not, a blue eye and sunken, which you have not, an unquestionable spirit, which you have not, a beard neglected, which you have not; but I pardon you for that, for simply your having in beard is a younger brother's revenue: then your hose should be ungartered, your bonnet unbanded, your sleeve unbuttoned, your shoe untied and everything about you demonstrating a careless desolation; but you are no such man; you are rather point-device in your accoutrements as loving yourself than seeming the lover of any other.

GLENN: *[As ORLANDO]* Fair youth, I would I could make thee believe I love.

ELLEN: *[As ROSALIND]* Me believe it! You may as soon make her that you love believe it; which, I warrant, she is apter to do than to confess she does: that is one of the points in which women still give the lie to their consciences. But, in good sooth, are you he that hangs the verses on the trees, wherein Rosalind is so admired?

GLENN: *[As ORLANDO]* I swear to thee, youth, by the white hand of Rosalind, I am that he, that unfortunate he.

ELLEN: *[As ROSALIND]* But are you so much in love as your rhymes speak?

GLENN: *[As ORLANDO]* Neither rhyme nor reason can express how much.

ELLEN: *[As ROSALIND]* Love is merely a madness, and, I tell you, deserves as well a dark house and a whip as madmen do: and the reason why they are not so punished and cured is, that the lunacy is so ordinary that the whippers are in love too. Yet I profess curing it by counsel.

GLENN: *[As ORLANDO]* Did you ever cure any so?

ELLEN: *[As ROSALIND]* Yes, one, and in this manner. He was to imagine me his love, his mistress; and I set him every day to woo me: at which time would I, being but a moonish youth, grieve, be effeminate, changeable, longing and liking, proud, fantastical, apish, shallow, inconstant, full of tears, full of smiles, for every passion something and for no passion truly any thing, as boys and women are for the most part cattle of this colour; would now like him, now loathe him; then entertain him, then forswear him; now weep for him, then spit at him; that I drave my suitor from his mad humour of love to a living humour of madness;

which was, to forswear the full stream of the world, and to live in a nook merely monastic. And thus I cured him; and this way will I take upon me to wash your liver as clean as a sound sheep's heart, that there shall not be one spot of love in't.

GLENN: *[As ORLANDO]* I would not be cured, youth.

ELLEN: *[As ROSALIND]* I would cure you, if you would but call me Rosalind and come every day to my cote and woo me.

GLENN: *[As ORLANDO]* Now, by the faith of my love, I will: tell me where it is.

ELLEN: *[As ROSALIND]* Go with me to it and I'll show it you and by the way you shall tell me where in the forest you live. Will you go?

GLENN: *[As ORLANDO]* With all my heart, good youth.

ELLEN: *[As ROSALIND]* Nay you must call me Rosalind. Come, sister, will you go?

GLENN: Yeah, well that was fantastic. Really very good, for a first go. There was obviously that bit where I kinda lost it, but basically, given the circumstances, I think it's gonna be great. *[He looks at his watch]* God, is that the time. I've gotta go. See you guys next week?

Glenn gathers up his music and rushes out.

ELLEN: *[Stunned]* And this has got to be ready with three rehearsals?

LANA: Two now!

They burst into laughter then catch themselves before beginning to pack up.

ELLEN: I'm Ellen.

LANA: Yeah, Glenn said you would be.

ELLEN: What? That's weird.

LANA: Glenn said that when you finally showed up your name would be Ellen.

ELLEN: What, so it wouldn't be Ellen before I showed up?

LANA: Not exactly.

ELLEN: It's certainly the first time I ever had to find my place while the rehearsal was actually going on.

LANA: You obviously don't fall asleep during rehearsals.

ELLEN: Not often, no.

LANA: Actually, you didn't do too badly.

ELLEN: It's a good piece.

LANA: Yeah. It appeals to melancholy Anglo-Celtic women.

ELLEN: That's me then?

LANA: You do have something of the Pre-Raphaelite about you.

ELLEN: But that's not you?

LANA: What do you think?

ELLEN: No. You are perhaps a little more burnt-out, washed-up in love.

LANA: Really?

ELLEN: You do look a little thwarted for someone obviously without responsibilities. I suppose some sentimental boy with a mother-complex made a mess of you and you never really got on your feet again.

LANA: He was in love with me and I was the one who ended up in analysis.

ELLEN: I suppose you never really made it up to his mother's expectations.

LANA: Not quite. Anyway, I scared him off.

ELLEN: And you have been hanging around all your former haunts "as ghosts are said to do".

LANA: Something like that. Anyway, what are you doing here? I didn't think Glenn's charm extended to any actor over twenty-one.

ELLEN: Perhaps he thinks I am twenty-one. Besides, don't you think Shakespeare is a good enough reason to get involved?

Act I – Scene 1

LANA: Do you like Shakespeare?

ELLEN: No. It's just that I am planning a romantic encounter. *As You Like It*'s good preparation for that. Or at least it seems to set it up nicely.

LANA: I thought that was Rachmaninov?

ELLEN: No. Rachmaninov is two nice people having tea in a railway cafeteria.

LANA: What's that?

ELLEN: *Brief Encounter*.

LANA: Never heard of him.

ELLEN: Never mind, it's just a daggy old film for melancholy Anglo-Celtic women.

LANA: Ah, condescension and self-deprecation in the same sentence – you're obviously not twenty-one. You'll probably bring me chicken soup next week.

ELLEN: Well, you'd better write my name down somewhere. Save you the embarrassment of trying to remember me next week.

LANA: No, I should remember. But that won't be enough to stop someone like you clamming up and pretending it never happened.

ELLEN: What never happened?

LANA: This half-baked and somewhat personal conversation.

ELLEN: You are very rude.

LANA: Not really. Haven't you noticed, from performing in these things, that everyone's instant friends and it's all kisses and hugs and impertinent, but vaguely insightful little banter sessions, like this. Then a week later, or the next time you work together, people seem to be struggling to remember your name, let alone that embarrassing little confession they coughed up between movements.

ELLEN: Is this an advanced apology or an accusation?

LANA: Neither. It's just a complaint about rehearsals.

ELLEN: Well, see how the other half lives. It's not just about rehearsals. Try being a thirty-something mother of two and see how many men remember your name, let alone the fact that they told you they were worried about being into little boys or something.

LANA: All right. Fair enough. For once let's concentrate on the names and no potentially embarrassing details. I'll try to forget about your romantic encounter!

ELLEN: And I'll forget about your boy with the mother complex.

LANA: What about the usual kisses and hugs?

ELLEN: Handshake.

They shake hands and LANA leaves stage right. A change of lighting indicates a change of location. After a few seconds thinking about what has just happened, ELLEN hears the sound of children playing stage left. She walks towards the children.

CHILD'S VOICE: Mummy!

As ELLEN is walking towards her children a teddy is tossed at her.

She catches it, takes a deep breath and continues walking.

End Scene.

Act 2 - Scene 1:

We see GLENN and LANA in rehearsal again the next Saturday working on the second song of the 'As You Like It' cycle. GLENN is at the piano.

LANA: *[As CELIA] [Sings]*
Under the greenwood tree,
Who loves to lie with me,
And turn his merry note
Unto the sweet bird's throat:
Come hither and see,
no enemy
But winter and rough weather.
Who doth ambition shun,
And loves to live i' th' sun
Seeking the food he eats,
And pleased with what he gets:
Come hither and see,
no enemy
But winter and rough weather.

ELLEN: *[As ROSALIND] [Entering in character]*
Never talk to me; I will weep.

LANA: *[As CELIA]* Do, I prithee; but yet have the grace to consider that tears do not become a man.

ELLEN: *[As ROSALIND]* But have I not cause to weep?

LANA: *[As CELIA]* As good cause as one would desire; therefore weep.

ELLEN: *[As ROSALIND]* His very hair is of the dissembling colour.

LANA: *[As CELIA]* Something browner than Judas's marry, his kisses are Judas's own children.

ELLEN: *[As ROSALIND]* I' faith, his hair is of a good colour.

LANA: *[As CELIA]* An excellent colour: your chestnut was ever the only colour.

ELLEN: *[As ROSALIND]* And his kissing is as full of sanctity as the touch of holy bread.

LANA: *[As CELIA]* He hath bought a pair of cast lips of Diana: a nun of winter's sisterhood kisses not more religiously; the very ice of chastity is in them.

ELLEN: *[As ROSALIND]* But why did he swear he would come this morning, and comes not?

LANA: *[As CELIA]* Nay, certainly, there is no truth in him.

ELLEN: *[As ROSALIND]* Do you think so?

LANA: *[As CELIA]* Yes; I think he is not a pick-purse nor a horse-stealer, but for his verity in love, I do think him as concave as a covered goblet or a worm-eaten nut.

ELLEN: *[As ROSALIND]* Not true in love?

LANA: *[As CELIA]* Yes, when he is in; but I think he is not in.

Act II – Scene 1

ELLEN: *[As ROSALIND]* You have heard him swear downright he was.

LANA: *[As CELIA]* 'Was' is not 'is:' besides, the oath of a lover is no stronger than the word of a tapster; they are both the confirmer of false reckonings. He attends here in the forest on the duke your father.

ELLEN: *[As ROSALIND]* I met the duke yesterday and had much question with him: he asked me of what parentage I was; I told him, of as good as he; so he laughed and let me go. But what talk we of fathers, when there is such a man as Orlando?

LANA: *[As CELIA]* O, that's a brave man! he writes brave verses, speaks brave words, swears brave oaths and breaks them bravely... But who comes here?

ELLEN: *[As ROSALIND]* Why, how now, Orlando! where have you been all this while? You a lover! And you serve me such another trick, never come in my sight more.

GLENN: *[As ORLANDO]* My fair Rosalind, I come within an hour of my promise. *[As GLENN]* OK. That's fine. Let's cut to the end bit. *[As ORLANDO]* With no less religion than if thou wert indeed my Rosalind: so adieu.

ELLEN: *[As ROSALIND]* Well, Time is the old justice that examines all such offenders, and let Time try: adieu.

GLENN moves to the piano.

LANA: *[As CELIA]* You have simply misused our sex in your love-prate: We must have you doublet and hose plucked over your head, and show the world what the bird hath done to her own nest

ELLEN: *[As ROSALIND]* O coz, coz, coz, my pretty little coz, that thou didst know how many fathom deep I am in love! But it cannot be sounded: my affection hath an unknown bottom, like the bay of Portugal.

LANA: *[As CELIA]* Or rather, bottomless, that as fast as you pour affection in, it runs out.

ELLEN: *[As ROSALIND]* No, that same wicked bastard of Venus that was begot of thought, conceived of spleen and born of madness, that blind rascally boy that abuses every one's eyes because his own are out, let him be judge how deep I am in love. I'll tell thee, Aliena, I cannot be out of the sight of Orlando: I'll go find a shadow and sigh till he come.

LANA: *[As CELIA]* And I'll sleep.

GLENN plays the scene to an end.

End scene.

Act 2 - Scene 2:

ELLEN and LANA are walking and talking. They have obviously been talking for a while and they are at ease, and almost cocky, with each other in a way that comes from working with someone on such a project. This is also an ease that comes from not knowing each other at all. Only should they get involved with each other's life would this ease and assurance fade. This is perhaps like the energy behind a one-night stand and is probably why they never really go into the practical details of life.

ELLEN: No, I've never performed it before. I've got a couple of videos of it and I get the script out every now and then and go over it. It's a great play.

LANA: Yeah, really. Anything to do with Shakespeare, I can never say no.

ELLEN: So, is that what you are doing your thesis on?

LANA: No. I kinda keep the performance stuff aside for fun. My thesis is pretty daggy – I am looking at the influence of Shakespeare on twentieth century composers.

ELLEN: Which ones?

LANA: Everyone really, Walton, Porter, Costello. But I'm also looking at the less obvious stuff. I really love it when you are listening to some dumbarse manufactured song on the radio and there's a line from *King Lear* or something.

ELLEN Yeah and what's really good about it is that you know that whoever's singing has absolutely no idea.

LANA: That's right, because the guy who wrote it never got to tell them.

ELLEN: If he ever got to meet them at all.

LANA: Exactly. He works in some building in LA and sits there all day reading Shakespeare until some record producer runs in and needs a track in ten minutes.

ELLEN: Great job.

LANA: Yeah.

ELLEN: I always think writing music for Shakespeare is a bit redundant, though. You should read Bernard Shaw. He talks about the way music is already fundamental to Shakespeare, so in that sense, you don't really need anything more.

LANA: Yeah, right. Cut to the Renaissance. "Hang on guys, let's not have a Renaissance 'cause they already did it in the 4th century BC." Are you really going to do without *West Side*?

Act II – Scene 2

ELLEN: God. That's so gay. You can always tell when someone's gay if they call it *West Side* and leave out the *Story*.

LANA: Yeah, maybe twenty years ago. It's Kylie now.

ELLEN: Yeah, well you brought her up.

LANA: Only in disparaging terms. Anyway that's all crap. The point is to find out what it all really means.

ELLEN: So what's your argument?

LANA: I don't have one at the moment.

ELLEN: Sounds promising.

LANA: It's going to take me about twenty years just to listen to all the music let alone try and understand it. And that's what is really difficult about it. Sitting down to listen to Duke Ellington, you don't want to write about it. And as soon as you do, you feel you have already lost the really good bit. And so you just luxuriate and wallow in the whole process and it's impossible to get anywhere.

ELLEN: It sounds to me like the project's in big trouble. I think you'd better go with the Bernard Shaw thesis and get the hell out of there.

LANA: Great. You must be really inspiring to your music students.

ELLEN: Don't be stupid. Teaching cello in the 'burbs isn't about inspiring anyone.

LANA: What is it about then?

ELLEN: It's about giving their parents something to brag about at dinner parties.

LANA: Is that what you give them?

ELLEN: It's what they want.

LANA: Yeah, their parents maybe. God you aren't melancholy, you're completely depressed.

ELLEN: Not completely, I hope. Although I am finding it harder to be as enthusiastic as I used to be. Do you ever get that person who comes up to you at parties and when you tell them what you do they say something like, "Wow that must be really fascinating." As if teaching brats is a kind of orgy of excitement.

LANA: Yeah, I know that one. That's why I never tell them that I do any teaching.

ELLEN: That's clever. I don't really deal with it very well these days. I used to get into it and carry on like teaching Brahms or playing Ravel is just one long drawn-out and fully funded state of ecstasy. Now I just tell them that all I really do is photocopying and filling in my BAS statement and then I just complain about not having any time to practise.

LANA: Is that how it is for you?

ELLEN: Sort of. Although I overdo it a bit to make the point. And then the poor accountant standing in front of me gets this vaguely disappointed

Act II – Scene 2

look on his face and I feel I've let him down. I know what they mean and they're right to think about it that way. It's just that something seems to be missing from it all now.

LANA: It's not missing, it's just that you are not working hard enough at it.

ELLEN: What do you mean?

LANA: Look, when you're fifteen it's all laid out in front of you. God, when you're fifteen you can't even brush your teeth without some bit of Beethoven jumping up and having it's way with you! But as you get older it's rarer and more special – like sex.

ELLEN: Speak for yourself.

LANA: Perhaps you have to work at it a little more.

ELLEN: Hang on. Are we talking about music or sex?

LANA: Is there a difference?

ELLEN: And what happens if it's not about that stuff becoming rarer? What if it's a matter of music, and our ability to really respond to music, actually being shut down and closed off by everything else that's going on around us?

LANA: You mean like adult life?

ELLEN: I'm not talking about responsibility – God, I've got two kids. I'm just thinking about all the stupid stuff that slides in between you and what

	you want to be thinking about. It's like a pane of glass inserted between you and what you want to be doing, what you want to be feeling.

LANA: That's what I mean about working harder.

ELLEN: But the Ravel *Piano Trio* doesn't change. Only we do. If a piece of music is going to ravish you while you are brushing your teeth at fifteen, why not at fifty?

LANA: Do you really want to be thinking about Ravel when you are brushing your falsies? I'm not sure that music doesn't change. It's not immune to the passions of its listeners. And it doesn't really have an obligation to ravish you either. If it comes easier as life gets more complicated I tend to be suspicious of it, anyway.

ELLEN: No pain, no gain?

LANA: Maybe. But it's always been about struggle and discomfort.

ELLEN: You're right. I just miss that feeling of being fully engaged. It's the most intensive experience I can remember.

LANA: You mean aside from giving birth.

ELLEN: Cut it out – you sound like my husband.

LANA: You say some pretty stupid things from time to time.

ELLEN: Such as?

LANA: I'm too polite to mention them.

They have arrived outside a café.

LANA: I'm starving. Do you want to have lunch?

ELLEN pauses thinking of nothing she'd rather do and everything she feels she must. Above all she tries hard not to say "no". Finally, she agrees as if she is saying "well I have to eat anyway".

ELLEN: Fine.

They sit at an outside table.

End scene.

Act 2 - Scene 3:

ELLEN and LANA are sitting in a café. They have been eating, drinking and talking for hours.

LANA: I remember it was in the summer. I think it was just after Christmas and everyone had gone to their families, so I had the place to myself. *[She pauses]* I had been out all day at a picnic with a bunch of complete strangers. I think someone I knew from uni had invited me, but when I showed up she wasn't there. I didn't really know her that well and I certainly didn't know her friends so, as I was there anyway, it didn't really matter to me who I had lunch with. It was a gorgeous, warm day. When she didn't show they asked me to stay and so I did. It's such a treat to be part of someone else's scene. You don't know anyone and no one knows you. You fit in because no one really has any reason for you not to. Or rather, you fit in because there's plenty of food and they need an extra person to play volleyball. You eat the food, you make up one side of the net and everyone's happy. *[She pauses]* Anyway, it had been a wonderful day. Those guys were lovely. When I got home the house was empty and I remember feeling really warm and, sort of, calm. I opened up the doors to let the breeze in and I sat down to play. I must have played for about two hours without really stopping. At one point though, I did stop because I, sort of, caught sight of myself. It was as though I had been playing unconsciously for ages and then I suddenly realised what I had been doing and I had stopped to let myself know how good it felt. I actually caught myself experiencing a moment of complete and unalloyed happiness. It wasn't just the playing, it was the whole day, the light in the corner of the room, the soda water in the fridge. There was nothing else to do but to go to sleep and to see if dreaming about it was any better.

ELLEN: You're very nostalgic.

LANA: Yes I am. But I think that what was so good about that day was that I felt a feeling like nostalgia as it was happening. That almost never happens to me. Even when I woke myself out of it, it was still there. Haven't you ever caught yourself in that kind of bliss moment?

ELLEN: Strangely enough it happened to me once – or actually twice – in a running race at the school sports in 1985.

LANA: Were you particularly good at athletics?

ELLEN: No, I was particularly bad. I hated sport at school. I got roped into because no one else was stupid enough to agree to do it. It was a 400-meter 'z' grade heat, or something, and I drew the outside lane. So there were about fifteen people behind me at the start and from the beginning of the race everyone in the stadium, including me, expected almost all of them to catch me up and run past me. Anyway the last thing I heard was the gun going off and after that I could only hear myself running. Panting like crazy – you know it's a long race especially when you are as unfit as I was, am. I didn't look behind me the whole time and after what seemed like ages, I ran across the line and I won the stupid race. The thing is I remember exactly how it felt. From the beginning I was totally alone and I had no sense of anyone else around me at all. I wasn't driven by any particular concern about anyone coming behind me – I didn't really care whether I won it or not. All I did was just concentrate on that single thing – and I didn't really think about that very much. In fact I don't remember thinking about anything at all. It was like what you said, everything just seemed to come together at a particular moment and everything just seemed to be in place.

LANA: Did you feel any sense of joy or elation about it?

ELLEN: It wasn't like that. It was more like a feeling of everything being absolutely right.

LANA: Did you feel it at the time?

ELLEN: I did. But what strengthened the feeling was that I had another go at it the next day. It was the 'z' grade final. Same race, same time, same outside lane and I did exactly the same thing.

LANA: I'm feeling a Jungian thing here.

ELLEN: Please! But it was a really great feeling. Doing it twice just gave me another glimpse at perfection.

Pause.

LANA: You know what's depressing though?

ELLEN: What?

LANA: I bet you have absolutely no idea how you did it.

ELLEN: None at all.

End scene.

Act 2 - Scene 4:

ELLEN and LANA are standing outside a café ready to leave. It is evening.

ELLEN: Which way do you go?

LANA: This way.

ELLEN: I go that way.

LANA: Fine. See you next week?

ELLEN: Yeah. Thanks for lunch.

LANA: You too.

ELLEN: Actually, Lana there was something you said before that seemed odd.

LANA: What?

ELLEN: You said you sat down to play that night. Don't you stand?

LANA: Not to play cello.

ELLEN: So you play cello too?

They stand looking at each other awkwardly. LANA moves and touches the scarf hanging over ELLEN's shoulder.

LANA: I am a cellist.

Awkwardly and then clinically ELLEN pecks her on the cheek and this has caught LANA by surprise. Not the emotion, just the action.

LANA: Bye.

ELLEN leaves. LANA waits awhile then turns and leaves.

End scene.

Act 2 - Scene 5:

ELLEN is standing in front of the bathroom mirror standing still and thinking. Everyone else in the house is still asleep. GLENN enters and they go straight into their characters.

ELLEN: *[As ROSALIND]* Did your brother tell you how I counterfeited to swoon when he showed me your handkerchief?

GLENN: *[As ORLANDO]* Ay, and greater wonders than that.

ELLEN: *[As ROSALIND]*
O, I know where you are: nay, 'tis true: for your brother and my sister no sooner met but they looked, no sooner looked but they loved, no sooner loved but they sighed, no sooner sighed but they asked one another the reason, no sooner knew the reason but they sought the remedy; and in these degrees have they made a pair of stairs to marriage which they will climb incontinent, or else be incontinent before marriage: they are in the very wrath of love and they will together; clubs cannot part them.

GLENN: *[As ORLANDO]*
They shall be married to-morrow, and I will bid the duke to the nuptial. But, O, how bitter a thing it is to look into happiness through another man's eyes! By so much the more shall I to-morrow be at the height of heart-heaviness, by how much I shall think my brother happy in having what he wishes for.

ELLEN: *[As ROSALIND]* Why then, to-morrow I cannot serve your turn for Rosalind?

GLENN: *[As ORLANDO]* I can live no longer by thinking.

ELLEN: *[As ROSALIND]*
I will weary you then no longer with idle talking. Know of me then, for now I speak to some purpose, that I know you are a gentleman of good conceit: I speak not this that you should bear a good opinion of my knowledge, insomuch I say I know you are; neither do I labour for a greater esteem than may in some little measure draw a belief from you, to do yourself good and not to grace me. Believe then, if you please, that I can do strange things: I have, since I was three year old, conversed with a magician, most profound in his art and yet not damnable. If you do love Rosalind so near the heart as your gesture cries it out, when your brother marries Aliena, shall you marry her: I know into what straits of fortune she is driven; and it is not impossible to me, if it appear not inconvenient to you, to set her before your eyes tomorrow human as she is and without any danger.

GLENN: *[As ORLANDO]* Speakest thou in sober meanings?

ELLEN: *[As ROSALIND]*
By my life, I do; which I tender dearly, though I say I am a magician. Therefore, put you in your best array: bid your friends; for if you will be married to-morrow, you shall, and to Rosalind, if you will.

Act II – Scene 5

Pause. They break out of character, but GLENN is only a figment of ELLEN's imagination, seemingly appearing in the mirror.

GLENN: That's a great dressing gown!

ELLEN: God. Who let you in?

GLENN: You did. Obviously.

ELLEN: What? I wasn't thinking about you.

GLENN: It's your imagination. Anyway, it doesn't matter. I'm here now.

ELLEN: What do you want?

GLENN: It's what you want that that we're here to discuss.

ELLEN: If I can't talk to Malcolm and, obviously, I can't talk to Lana, why on Earth would I talk to you?

GLENN: Darling, you've got to talk to someone or you'll burst. Besides, if you don't talk to anyone the whole thing will be far less enjoyable and it will fade quicker. There's nothing like complete discretion to kill a fantasy.

ELLEN: Complete discretion is one thing. Bouncing about on your web page is another.

GLENN: Do you honestly think there's anything on my web page about anyone other than me?

ELLEN: That's true. But can I really trust you?

GLENN: This is not really very flattering, you know. But when you think about it, I'm the only one you can trust at the moment.

ELLEN: Why is that?

GLENN: I'm the only one who has a specific interest in keeping you happy.

ELLEN: Apart from Malcolm.

GLENN: Yeah, right. Look, I need you on side because I want the Shakespeare gig to go smoothly.

ELLEN: So you mean that, within the context of your completely self-serving attitude, I can rely on your ultimate discretion?

GLENN: Something like that.

ELLEN: I suppose that's fair enough.

GLENN: So, what's the situation?

ELLEN: I like her.

GLENN: That's obvious. Why?

ELLEN: She's funny. She's really talented... I don't know, she's...

GLENN: I can see this is going to set poets reeling.

ELLEN: What do you want?

GLENN: Stop asking me what I want.

ELLEN:	Well, I only just met her. How do I know what she's like.
GLENN:	That's not what I asked. What I asked was, why do you like her?
ELLEN:	Perhaps I don't really know.
GLENN:	You're the one who's thinking of sleeping with her.
ELLEN:	Hang on. Who said anything about sleeping with her?
GLENN:	Is everything OK at home?
ELLEN:	Apart from the fact that Hector wakes up three times a night and Imogen's got conjunctivitis – everything's fine.
GLENN:	How are things with Malcolm?
ELLEN:	Absolutely fine. We never really get enough time together but that's what it's like with kids. We do OK.
GLENN:	No problems in the sex department?
ELLEN:	No problems there, I can assure you.
GLENN:	I'm not the one who needs assurance.
ELLEN:	And you think I do?
GLENN:	I think you're covering up something.
ELLEN:	I'm not. I have just got a thing about this girl.

GLENN: What sort of thing?

ELLEN: Don't be so practical. Haven't you ever met someone and just fallen for them? I don't mean fallen in love with them. But just fallen for their line. I met her and I immediately found her really interesting. Sure we had all the "do you know this?", "do you like that?" and "yeah same" stuff but that's not really what I'm talking about.

GLENN: So what is it about Lana? Do you want to sleep with her?

ELLEN: I don't think so. At least, I'm not thinking about sex so much. But then again I kind of want her. I'd really like to just get her into a hotel room for a weekend and see what happens.

GLENN: I know what would happen. So why don't you ask her?

ELLEN: I don't really know. It's complicated. I suppose I am afraid of hurting my husband and my kids. But in a sense, if I was dragged along the road and it all happened in secret I'd probably get over it. I suppose what I am really afraid of is the effect on me. It's not just a guilt thing, although that would be part of it. It's also about the impact of engagement with another person. I just feel that my life is so full of my own stuff, the kids and Malcolm, that the idea of taking on anyone's else's stuff is too overwhelming. So I kind of let it lie.

GLENN: And what does that feel like?

Act II – Scene 5

ELLEN: Awful. I think about her all the time. I daydream. I see her coming out of every building and every time I get an email or a phone call I expect it to be Lana. Of course it never is.

GLENN: Does she know about it?

ELLEN: I doubt it. At least not the daydreaming. Except sometimes I think to myself, how could she not know about it? I feel so obvious. And sometimes I get the feeling she feels exactly the same way. You know she says things? But when I really think about it, I just think she has no idea and no particular interest in me. I mean she probably thinks I'm some sort of joke.

GLENN: Are you unhappy?

ELLEN: No. I'm really happy. But then again I know I'm going to be unhappy.

GLENN: Are you sure things are OK with Malcolm and the kids?

ELLEN: God, when did you get so family friendly? That's all fine. I have nothing to complain about. I know it sounds like some sort of blokey cliché, but it really has nothing to do with them. I'm not unsatisfied, I'm not bored, we're sexually active and my kids are fantastic.

GLENN: I assume you mean you and your husband are sexually active and that your kids are just generally fantastic.

ELLEN: Of course. I mean, do married people only get interested in other people if they're unhappy? Am I the only woman in the world who is happily married but still thinks actively about having sex with other people? I bet men do it all the time - and talk about it all the time – but no one says anything about it. No one questions their relationships.

GLENN: So there's nothing wrong with your marriage?

ELLEN: If there is I can't see it. I'm just mad about this girl. It's driving me nuts, but I don't know what to do about it.

GLENN: So what do you do about it?

ELLEN: Oh, I just faff around from one encounter to the next. Putting my life on hold for something that will never really happen.

GLENN: Why don't you just tell her? Or tell your husband?

ELLEN: What purpose is that going to serve?

GLENN: It will break the circuit. Either she'll love the idea or she'll back off. Or Malcolm will make you feel so bad about it that you'll back off.

ELLEN: Doesn't that seem to you just a little indulgent?

GLENN: It's less indulgent than getting drunk one night after rehearsal and accidentally going to bed with her.

ELLEN: That's not what I was planning at all. Anyway, that's not indulgence, it's negligence.

GLENN: You think so, do you? Anyway telling either of them is certainly risky.

ELLEN: Why, do you think Malcolm will leave me?

GLENN: It's possible I suppose, but it's unlikely. No, I was thinking more about the risk that Lana might actually like the idea and that you might be forced to get involved with her. And where would that leave your 'brief encounter'?

ELLEN: It's probably more likely that she's just some frivolous bitch who gets turned on by the idea of sleeping with a married woman.

GLENN: That is a bit harsh. She's probably worried that you are some bi-curious little twit who wants a break from dick.

ELLEN: Hang on, you are giving her a bit too much cred, aren't you?

GLENN: My God, you are patronising her already! Yes I am giving her "a bit too much cred", but only if you see her as some sort of fantasy girl for you to project on.

ELLEN: Perhaps I do.

GLENN: Don't you think that's a little bit silly?

ELLEN: I suppose so. But she's like this single chick – obviously without particularly responsibilities and I'm... well...

GLENN: A mother?

ELLEN: Does that sound infantilising?

GLENN: Um. Yeah. God, you give Hector more emotional maturity and he's only five.

ELLEN: Seven and a half actually.

GLENN: See what I mean? Look, I know you. When you were twenty-five and you started teaching undergraduates, you used to say that they were young and stupid and that they didn't know anything. Now that you are thirty-five and domesticated you are saying the same thing about single people. So do they ever get to the point on the Ellen scale of emotional and intellectual maturity when they get to speak for themselves?

ELLEN: When they agree with me.

GLENN: Exactly.

ELLEN: So what do you think Lana would say if I let her speak for herself?

GLENN: It could be anything. She probably likes you – why else would she spend all that time with you? She asked you to lunch.

ELLEN: But if I know anything about swinging singles, it's that they have bravado!

GLENN: I know. Don't you love it!

ELLEN: No. I wish they wouldn't.

GLENN:	That wouldn't help you. What you don't want them to have is feelings. Particularly for you. Has it ever occurred to you that she might feel exactly the way you do?
ELLEN:	How?
GLENN:	Scared, inadequate and vulnerable.
ELLEN:	But if she felt like that, wouldn't she just avoid me?
GLENN:	You don't avoid her. Anyway I'm out of here. I've got that Bernard Shaw thing!
ELLEN:	What about this Shakespeare thing?
GLENN:	You know me, Darling. *[Lights fade on him]* Ciao. *[He sings]* "All I want is a room somewhere, far away from the cold night air..."

End scene.

Act 3 - Scene 1:

It is the following Saturday morning in the entrance hall of ELLEN's house. ELLEN is bundling Malcolm and the brood (offstage) into the car and seeing them off for a weekend in the country at Gran's..

ELLEN: Hang on.

She runs across the room and grabs the teddy.

ELLEN: You forgot this.

She throws it off stage. As we hear them drive off she waves them goodbye and wipes a little wisp of a tear. Straightening herself up, walks halfway across the stage to grab her bags. Suddenly she stops, thinks and makes a gesture of triumph, partly with the joy of a weekend off, partly anticipating what might happen when the family are away.

End scene.

Act 3 - Scene 2:

Later that morning in the rehearsal space, the final rehearsal is not going well.

ELLEN: Oh my faith it has gone,
Running free from my scorn,
And my heart shares a bed with repulsion.

There's a stench in the air.
Foolish lovers despair,
And my song sounds a note of revulsion.

But who can relieve my sorrow?
My vanity longs for tomorrow.
Most friendship is feigning, most loving mere folly;
Then sing, hey-ho, O sing, hey-ho the holly.

GLENN: Considering we're doing that tomorrow, I think we are in a bit of trouble. Anyway can't be helped.

ELLEN: Don't you think we had better do it again?

GLENN: I can't. I have got to be somewhere else until about four.

LANA: Could we do it then?

GLENN: Can't get the space.

ELLEN: *[Jumping in]* We could rehearse at my place. I mean Malcolm and the kids aren't there.

GLENN: How long could we go.

ELLEN: All night if we have to. They don't get back until the concert tomorrow.

GLENN: OK see you at four.

ELLEN: Right.

ELLEN and LANA are left behind as GLENN bustles out (as they were in Act One, Scene One). This time they say nothing.

End scene.

Act 3 - Scene 3:

Later that afternoon ELLEN is buzzing around getting the house ready for the other two (but really LANA) to rehearse in. She madly clears away all the toys strewn over the house, the high chairs, and the kids' clothes drying by the heater and tries to make it look as much like a bachelorette's pad as a five-bedroom house in the inner city can look. She closes the kids' bedroom doors and puts the family photos behind those of her parents and friends taken in the 1980s. Then she thinks this a little pathetic and so replaces the family photos in pride of place and even puts the parents and friends away in a drawer where they belong. While she is opening the kids' bedroom doors again, she hears GLENN on the answering machine saying he is not going to make it. She does not race to pick up the phone but listens to the answering machine where, as soon as he has hung up, she wipes the message. Catching sight of a photo of Malcolm with the kids, she races into one of their rooms, grabs a couple of teddies and tosses them on the couch just before LANA (we presume) knocks at the door. LANA and ELLEN enter the sitting room.

LANA: I'm sorry I'm late.

ELLEN: No. You're not. I mean, Glenn's not even here yet.

LANA: Oh, right.

LANA sits on the couch while ELLEN buzzes around.

ELLEN: Do you want something to drink?

LANA: No thanks. I'm fine.

ELLEN: I'll have one I think.

She pours half a glass of wine and gulps in down nervously.

LANA: Is everything OK? You seem a bit edgy.

ELLEN: No. I'm fine. I mean, I've been running around. God, the place was in a mess and I just need to... anyway... you don't want to know...

ELLEN is babbling and LANA knows it.

LANA: This place is great.

ELLEN: Yeah it's fantastic. They've done a great job. It's amazing what they can do nowadays...

LANA: You mean you've done a great job?

ELLEN: Me? No it was really Malcolm and his architect, I really kept out of it, you know. I suppose he's the lawyer.

LANA: What, did you have problems with council?

ELLEN: No. Just the usual financial issues. What I mean is... well, you know, my salary's not going to build this.

LANA: Do you and your husband keep your money separate?

ELLEN: No. We don't.

LANA: So, it's your money too, isn't it?

ELLEN: Yes. It is. I just meant that. Oh I see what you mean. Yes I agree. A woman does really have the right to consider her husband's income as her own. I mean, what about all that unpaid work that women do. You know I really hate how some people just think that because some men have these huge paying jobs in the city that the wife just sits at home waiting for hubby to dole out the pocket money. I totally agree. I'm not that sort of person at all. True, we do lead our own lives and we're free to... but I just think that if people are going to...Weren't we supposed to be avoiding this kind of conversation?

LANA: Are you sure you are all right? You seem really nervous.

ELLEN: I'm fine. *[Slowing herself down]* Would you just excuse me a minute?

LANA: Yeah.

ELLEN: I just need to go to the...

LANA: Fine.

ELLEN moves downstage as if into her bathroom, as in Act Two Scene Five. She talks to the mirror.

ELLEN: Just get a grip. You're going crazy. *[She takes a deep breath]* This is stupid. Just tell her and get it over and done with. If she's interested, deal with it then. If she hates the idea she'll leave. No, but... Oh, God. Just do it! How long have I been in here? She'll think that I...

ELLEN rushes back into the sitting room area up stage and sits on the couch with LANA.

ELLEN: Sorry about that. Ah, I am a bit nervous to tell you the truth. I don't know how to say this because it's a long time since I...

Lana's mobile rings.

LANA: I'll just see who this is? Oh, it's Glenn. *[Answering]* Hi Glenn. *[Listening]* Yeah, I'm here already. *[Listening]* Oh hell. *[Listening]* But do you think we can pull it off without rehearsing this arvo? *[Listening]* All right, OK. *[Listening]* Maybe an hour before we said? *[Listening]* Fine. See you.

ELLEN: What's happening?

LANA: He's not coming. He says he left a message on your answering machine.

ELLEN: What? When?

Act III – Scene 3

LANA: About fifteen minutes ago.

ELLEN: That's odd. I didn't hear it. Are you sure? You know Glenn.

LANA: Yeah, well he's not coming anyway. So I suppose I had better go. You'll have things to do.

ELLEN: Yes. I mean, no... I suppose there's no use us working on it.

LANA: Probably not much use without Glenn. I really should go anyway.

ELLEN: Fine.

LANA get up and walks towards the door. ELLEN follows.

ELLEN: I'm sorry I didn't get the message. I could have called you.

LANA: That's fine. I probably would have been on my way anyway.

Soon she is standing on the front step.

ELLEN: So I suppose I'll see you tomorrow?

LANA: Yeah. Let's hope for a miracle.

ELLEN: I think that's what we need.

LANA: See you then. *[She is off and then she turns back.]* Ellen?

ELLEN: Yes?

LANA: Did you actually hear Glenn's message on the answering machine?

ELLEN: Yes. I mean, yes I didn't get the message. Sorry.

LANA: No. I... just... thought it was odd... *[Laughs nervously]*... Never mind. I'll see you tomorrow.

ELLEN: I'm sorry about it, Lana.

LANA: See ya.

ELLEN sees her off and stands there wanting the ground to swallow her up.

End scene.

Act 4 - Scene 1:

ELLEN, GLENN and LANA are performing the final song of the show in a concert hall before a big audience. If we could read their thoughts we would see that this is what happens the day after the night before in which nothing happened..

LANA: I once sang long songs of sorrow,
I once wrote short tales of pain,
I had a place within my heart,
I kept it just the same.

I now sing no songs of sorrow
I spurn to hear tales of pain,
I found a place within my heart,
I call her Rosalaine

So sing me no songs of sorrow,
And tell me no tales of pain,
I keep a place within my heart
I call her Rosalaine

LANA: *[As CELIA]* O my poor Rosalind, whither wilt thou go?
Wilt thou change fathers? I will give thee mine.
I charge thee, be not thou more grieved than I am.

ELLEN: *[As ROSALIND]* I have more cause.

LANA: *[As CELIA]* Thou hast not, cousin;
Prithee be cheerful: know'st thou not, the duke
Hath banish'd me, his daughter?

ELLEN: *[As ROSALIND]* That he hath not.

LANA: *[As CELIA]* No, hath not? Rosalind lacks then the love
Which teacheth thee that thou and I am one:
Shall we be sunder'd? shall we part, sweet girl?
No: let my father seek another heir.
Therefore devise with me how we may fly,
Whither to go and what to bear with us;
And do not seek to take your change upon you,
To bear your griefs yourself and leave me out;
For, by this heaven, now at our sorrows pale,
Say what thou canst, I'll go along with thee.

ELLEN: *[As ROSALIND]* Why, whither shall we go?

LANA: *[As CELIA]* To seek my uncle in the forest of Arden.

ELLEN: *[As ROSALIND]* Alas, what danger will it be to us,
Maids as we are, to travel forth so far!
Beauty provoketh thieves sooner than gold.

LANA: *[As CELIA]* I'll put myself in poor and mean attire
And with a kind of umber smirch my face;
The like do you: so shall we pass along
And never stir assailants.

ELLEN: *[As ROSALIND]* Were it not better,
Because that I am more than common tall,
That I did suit me all points like a man?

Act IV – Scene 1

> A gallant curtle-axe upon my thigh,
> A boar-spear in my hand; and--in my heart
> Lie there what hidden woman's fear there will–
> We'll have a swashing and a martial outside,
> As many other mannish cowards have
> That do outface it with their semblances.

LANA: *[As CELIA]* What shall I call thee when thou art a man?

ELLEN: *[As ROSALIND]* I'll have no worse a name than Jove's own page;
And therefore look you call me Ganymede.
But what will you be call'd?

LANA: *[As CELIA]* Something that hath a reference to my state
No longer Celia, but Aliena.... Let's away,
And get our jewels and our wealth together,
Devise the fittest time and safest way
To hide us from pursuit that will be made
After my flight. Now go we in content
To liberty and not to banishment. *[Exeunt]*

End scene.

Act 4 - Scene 2:

> *GLENN, ELLEN and LANA are packing up backstage. GLENN hands ELLEN an envelope and kisses her goodbye.*

GLENN: Here's your cash, darling! I've got to go, big kisses, you were fantastic! *[To LANA]* Bye sweetie. I'll send you the script next week and you can let me know. *[He exits]*

LANA: Bye Glenn.

> *LANA and ELLEN are alone for a second. LANA puts out her hand to ELLEN. She kisses LANA on the cheek but the moment falls flat. Suddenly we hear:*

CHILD'S VOICE: *[Off]* Mummy!

> *Again the teddy is tossed at ELLEN. She catches it and looks at LANA.*

ELLEN: I'm coming darling.

> *ELLEN walks offstage throwing open her arms as if about to catch her kids.*
>
> *LANA stands there alone a minute before the lights fade.*
>
> *Curtain.*

www.ingramcontent.com/pod-product-compliance
Lightning Source LLC
Chambersburg PA
CBHW071318080526
44587CB00018B/3272